Ann LOVE & JANE DRAKE

Trash Action*

A FRESH LOOK at GARBAGE

Illustrated by **Mark Thurman**

Tundra Books

To our recycling heroes, who've made a difference one carrot peel at a time: Ruth Drake Alloway, Henry Barnett, Kathleen Barnett, Doreen Barnett, Judy Barnett, Fran Barnett, Tony Barrett, Jennifer Cayley, Jane Falconi, Ray Fletcher, Bart Hall, Wally and Mona Livingstone, Geoff Love, Peter Love, Gage Love, Donna O'Connor, Luke Racine, and Harold Smith.
A.L. and J.D.

To those who see that everything on planet Earth, our home, is connected.
M.T.

Text copyright © 2006 by Ann Love and Jane Drake
Illustrations copyright © 2006 by Mark Thurman

Published in Canada by Tundra Books,
75 Sherbourne Street, Toronto, Ontario M5A 2P9

Published in the United States by Tundra Books of Northern New York,
P.O. Box 1030, Plattsburgh, New York 12901

Library of Congress Control Number: 200527009

Library and Archives Canada Cataloguing in Publication

Love, Ann
Trash action : a fresh look at garbage / Ann Love, Jane Drake ; Mark Thurman, illustrator.

ISBN 0-88776-721-4

1. Refuse and refuse disposal – Juvenile literature. 2. Recycling (Waste, etc.) – Juvenile literature. 3. Consumption (Economics) – Juvenile literature. I. Drake, Jane II. Thurman, Mark, 1948- III. Title.

TD792.L69 2006   j363.72'88   C2005-902893-9

ONTARIO ARTS COUNCIL
CONSEIL DES ARTS DE L'ONTARIO

We acknowledge the financial support of the Government of Canada through the Book Publishing Industry Development Program (BPIDP) and that of the Government of Ontario through the Ontario Media Development Corporation's Ontario Book Initiative. We further acknowledge the support of the Canada Council for the Arts and the Ontario Arts Council for our publishing program.

Medium: Watercolor and colored pencil on paper

Text design: Sari Naworynski

ISBN-13: 978-0-88776-721-0
ISBN-10: 0-88776-721-4

Printed in Canada

This book is printed on acid-free paper that is 100% recycled, ancient-forest friendly (100% post-consumer recycled).

1 2 3 4 5 6   11 10 09 08 07 06

Contents

Acknowledgments

The authors would like to thank Frank Amaral; Bob Argue; Ian Barnett; Kim Bilous; Ken Brock; Gregory Bryce; Kathy and Bob Clay; Barbara and Dawn Cochrane; Jane Crist; Richard Dixon; Christa Domchek; Brian, Jim, Madeline, and Stephanie Drake; Ron Dueck; Pete Ewins; Elaine and Sam Flanigan; Miriam Geitz; Monte Hummel; Adele Hurley; Ditta Kasdan; Jaan Koel; Todd Kostal; Aiden, Max, and Thea Lauzon; Susan Leppington; Mary Ann and Rob Lewis; Adrian, David, Jennifer, and Melanie Love; Anne Mathewson; Bill McCaig; Phil Mosley; Mark Newman; Eliza Olsen; Olivia Racine; John Riley; Kathleen Roberts; Mark Rudolph; Mark and Mason Salmoni; Aaron Smith; Ian Taylor; Mary Thompson; Phyllis Vernon; and Mindy Willett.

Thanks also to family and friends who have lent their fine photographs: Tom Drake (page 22), Rob Lewis (page 56), David Love (pages 5, 8, 34, 49), and Kate Love (page 54).

Special thanks to Geoff Love, Janet Robins, Anne Wheatley, and Bill Rees, who offered their professional advice and valuable time. Thanks again to the *re*markable and *re*sponsive staff at Tundra Books. It is *re*warding to collaborate with Kathy Lowinger and our editor, Sue Tate, who can *re*work and *re*word with *re*spect and *re*ason.

NATURE'S WAY

"Re"-Thinking

It's a fabulous morning – a day to spend outside. It's going to warm up for sure. You gulp down your juice and cereal and take a moment to stuff a water bottle, energy bar, and apple into your backpack. But you leave your jacket hanging on the hook. And forget the bike – you feel like a good leg-stretching walk, listening to your favorite tunes through your cool new earphones.

As you step onto the sidewalk, a diesel truck passes by, belching gases and fumes. You hold your breath and, when you inhale again, the smell is gone. But what if the breeze didn't sweeten the air? What if the trees didn't process the carbon dioxide in that exhaust and release fresh oxygen for you to breathe?

Music fills your ears and gets your mind jumping. What if you couldn't count on the weather? What if you couldn't count on spring coming, or any of the seasons? That would throw everything off – maybe, even, what's for breakfast.

You take a sip of water and tear open the energy bar. Its thick cardboard lining slips onto the ground. You bend to pick it up and look around for a trash can, then remember there's a recycling box at school. That's where you'll put it. It's the least you can do for planet Earth.

If you feel part of the natural world and want to support it, read on. This book will help you measure how much Nature you use every day. Because you control what you consume and what you throw away, it will take a hard look at garbage. Special sections will bring you up to date on where we are with pre-cycling and the three R's – reducing, reusing, and recycling – as well as landfill, incineration, and new technologies. You'll read about ancient garbage and new twists on the age-old problem of litter. You'll track the connections between you, your lifestyle, your garbage, and your planet – and why your choices to buy less and consume less will make a real difference and help your world.

Get ready to "re"-think your relationship with Nature.

HEY! I'M **ROLLY**. I'M REALLY INTO *RE*-WORDS – *REDUCE, REUSE, RECYCLE, RE. . . .*

CALL ME **CAN-IT**. I TALK TRASH ALL THE TIME.

BRIGHT BULB'S MY NAME. I SHED NEW LIGHT ON GARBAGE.

YOUR ECOLOGICAL FOOTPRINT

Big Feet

Imagine walking barefoot along a beach, always keeping your steps on the wet sand where the waves wash up onshore. With each step, you leave a clear print; but when you look back, the water washes your footprints away. The fresh unmarked sandy beach reappears. Your human footprint seems insignificant compared to the power of Nature. But is it?

Your feet touch the earth all the time. In the 1990s, scientists in Canada, Dr. William Rees and Mathis Wackernagel, developed the idea of an "ecological footprint" to measure the mark people leave on Nature. They added up all the areas on Earth that are biologically productive – areas that

* grow green plants, trees, and crops;
* supply fresh water;
* produce energy for heat and transportation;
* provide materials for shelter;
* naturally absorb waste.

Then they divided that by the number of people on Earth. They found there were 1.9 hectares (4.7 acres), about the area of five soccer fields, for each person if we all had an equal share. When they accounted for the millions of wildlife species on Earth, they trimmed back to 1.5 hectares (3.7 acres) per person. They said that if all people had an ecological footprint of 1.5 hectares, we would leave no permanent marks on Earth and Nature could recover each year, just like wet sand on a beach.

How much Nature do humans actually use? The footprint team (Rees and Wackernagel, who published *Our Ecological Footprint: Reducing Human Impact on the Earth* with New Society Publishers in 1996) compared different countries and cities and counted up

* all the food eaten;
* water, materials, and energy consumed;
* transportation used;
* ground built upon;
* garbage created.

They found that Canada, the United States, and many western European countries leave ecological footprints that are more than three times their fair share. If everyone on Earth had such big feet, the air, water, and soil humans need to survive couldn't refresh and recover each year.

If you live in a country with an oversized ecological footprint, chances are your personal footprint is too big. Since Nature provides everything we need

and takes in all the waste we produce, it makes sense to keep our footprints within Nature's limits.

One way to reduce your ecological footprint is to cut back on garbage, which involves much more than what you throw away. Garbage starts when you choose an item, includes how you use it, how you care for it, as well as how you dispose of it.

Wasted!

What happens when people take more from Nature than they give back?
History tells us. Archaeologists think oversized ecological footprints caused the
collapse of some ancient civilizations, including the

* Mayans of Central America;
* Mound Builders of the Mississippi Valley;
* Khmer of Angkor in Cambodia;
* Statue Builders of Easter Island;
* Anasazi of the American Southwest.

Here are two of their stories.

The Statue Builders of Easter Island

Land ahoy! In 1722, western ships first anchored off this remote South Pacific
island. Dutch Admiral Jacob Roggeveen recorded what he found in a journal.

He saw islanders bowing down and worshipping gigantic stone figures
called moai. Hundreds of look-alike moai – some as tall as 10 meters (32 feet)
and weighing 81 metric tons (89 tons) – faced inland, as if watching the island's
people. Because the island was treeless and without any material to make
sturdy ropes, the admiral couldn't imagine how the statues were erected onto
their stone platforms.

About fifty years later, Captain Cook landed on Easter Island and found far
fewer people – most of them hungry – and many of the moai toppled. By the
early twentieth century, only 111 native Easter Islanders survived.

Archaeologists have tried to piece together what happened. They believe the
island was uninhabited until about 400 A.D., when Polynesians landed in
dugout canoes. The settlers brought seeds to plant, chickens for eggs, and rats
for meat. From studying old pollen grains, scientists know that when the
Polynesians arrived, the lowlands were covered with huge palm forests.

It was a tropical paradise. People fished in the sea, harvested eggs from
seabird colonies, cut trees, and grew crops. They carved their moai from the
walls of an extinct volcano and used tree trunks to roll the statues around the
island.

By 1550 A.D. there were over 10,000 people on Easter Island and over 900 moai. Soon, most of the seabirds became extinct – no more bird eggs to eat – and the forests were gone. The introduced rats loved eating palm nuts, so the trees did not reseed after logging. Without trees to hold the topsoil, much of it washed into the sea and the crops began to fail. Without trees, people could not build boats to fish offshore. They became hungry, warred among themselves, and toppled their moai. The population declined sharply and some islanders resorted to cannibalism. Then slave ships arrived and kidnapped many of the survivors. Without trees, people could not build boats to escape their lost, wasted paradise.

The Anasazi of Chaco Canyon

In the 1970s, botanist Julio Betancourt scanned the ridges around Chaco Canyon, New Mexico, and wondered why there were no trees. He knew that hardy pinyon pine and juniper trees usually grow in high desert country.

On the canyon floor below, he could see the ruins of massive stone buildings, called great houses, erected by the Anasazi between 850 A.D. and 1120 A.D. The largest originally stood four stories high and contained over 650 rooms. It was framed with logs from forests 120 km (74 mi.) away. The Anasazi had not invented the wheel nor had they domesticated animals to carry heavy loads – the stones and timber were all lugged by human muscle and sweat.

Beside the ruins of the great houses still lie the remains of stone dams and canals, constructed to channel rainwater to thousands of gardens that once grew corn, squash, and beans. And radiating in all directions from the canyon are hundreds of miles of smoothed paths, some as wide as a modern two-lane highway. Despite all this labor and careful construction, the Anasazi abandoned the canyon by 1150 A.D., during a prolonged drought. The question scientists kept asking was, why would people construct a monumental community in this dry, tree-less canyon in the first place?

In a crevice near the ruins, Dr. Betancourt spotted an old pack-rat nest containing pine needles. He knew that pack rats don't travel far to collect scraps, so he took the nest back to his lab. In carbon dating tests, he found the nest was 1,200 years old. This proved that pine trees must have grown close to the nest in 800 A.D.

Other scientists dug into old trash dumps and found many deer bones from the time the Anasazi first came to the canyon. But, as years passed, the deer bones disappeared and gopher bones increased. It seems the Anasazi ate all the deer and had to kill smaller animals for meat.

Scientists believe the Anasazi must have cut down all the trees for firewood and to frame their first great houses. They then had to walk longer distances to find wood. And without living tree roots to draw underground water up to the surface, water became scarce in the canyon. Meanwhile, the meat supply was disappearing. When the rains didn't come, there wasn't enough water to irrigate the corn. There wasn't even enough water to drink.

Today, while the canyon no longer supports great houses and large numbers of people, it is still home to pack rats, lizards, and other creatures of the desert. Nature survived, but an Anasazi city could not.

Waste Watching:
Your Garbage and Your Footprint

Do you have any idea how big your garbage footprint is? And what kind of waste you create? Start with your bedroom. What do you throw out? How often do you empty your wastebasket?

What about garbage in other parts of your house – the kitchen, family room, bathroom? How about the garden? As gross as it sounds, can you name the kinds and amounts of waste you make?

A typical North American family's household garbage bags are about
* one-third organics (food scraps, garden trimmings);
* one-third paper products (cardboard, newspapers, fine papers);
* one-fifth metals, glass, and plastics;
* the rest, a mishmash of old clothes, carpets, shoes, bedding, sofas, chairs, cabinets, computers, radios, tires, dry- wall, lumber, flooring, pet hair, dust, batteries, household cleaners, paint, and so on....

If you live in Canada, the United States, or Western Europe, chances are your household creates close to one ton of garbage a year. If you count the waste created in extracting, manufacturing, trans- porting, and using what you throw away, your family could be linked to more than 18 metric tons (20 tons) each year. Multiply that by all the people in your community and you can see why garbage is an enormous part of oversized footprints.

Any waste that is reused or recycled cuts back on the amount Nature has to absorb. And the more you stop wasting in the first place, the more you reduce your mark on Nature. "Re"-thinking garbage can trim your oversized ecological footprint.

And lots of people are "re"-thinking. The city of Toronto has run a curbside blue box program for many years. At first, families sorted glass bottles, metal cans, plastic bottles, newspapers, and cardboard from their regular garbage for recycling. After the success of the blue box, the city added a gray box for newspapers, cardboard, and household paper waste, including fine paper, junk mail, and flyers. Then, in 2004, the city gave a green bin (see page 36) to households for biodegradables. Those households still carry nearly a metric ton (1 ton) of waste to their curbsides a year, but well over half is sorted and recovered for recycling and composting.

TOTAL HOUSEHOLD WASTE GENERATED	PERCENT RECOVERED FOR RECYCLING/COMPOSTING
38.6% organics	70%
34.5% paper fibers	80%
9.3% plastics	75%
5.1% glass	88%
3.4% metal	72%
9.0% other waste materials	0%
0.1% household hazardous waste	0%

Monster Bear — A Gitksan Story

In their stories, Gitksan elders of northern British Columbia taught their people to respect Nature, including animals, parts of animals, and even animal waste. Although they never talked about ecological footprints, the elders understood the concept. This old story shows they knew that respecting waste and avoiding wastefulness are hard lessons to learn.

The great Chief-in-Heaven gave the lush and beautiful land of Temlaxam, which lies between the Nass and Skeena Rivers in British Columbia, to the

Gitksan. The salmon were so plentiful in its rivers that people could catch them in baskets. The mountain lakes teemed with trout and the cedar forests abounded with wildlife – gathering and hunting food was easy. Even so, the elders cautioned the people to treat wildlife with respect or face punishment from Nature.

In one mountain lake near Temlaxam lived a monster bear with radiant golden brown fur. The bear never bothered the young people who fished for trout in the lake or picked blueberries along its shores. The young people always prepared their fish by filleting the flesh off the bones and casting aside the tail attached to the skeleton. Then they cooked the fillets and ate the fish with wild blueberries.

One night, the young women noticed how beautifully the scales on the waste tails shimmered in the moonlight. They wrapped the fish bones around their heads so the tails rested on their foreheads, like frontlets on a headdress. Then they danced under the stars with the scales sparkling.

They enjoyed themselves so much, the young people started to fish just to make headdresses. They threw away the fish fillets and danced the night away.

The bear grew angry that the trout from the lake were being mocked and wasted. It surfaced in a rage and attacked all the young people dancing on the shore. The young people fought the bear, but their arrows only dangled from its golden brown back, not breaking through the thick skin. Most of the young dancers died.

Yet the survivors did not learn. A group returned to the lake, caught trout, and made headdresses. They danced and laughed until the bear rose again from the lake and killed a young woman.

When her two brothers learned of her death, they plotted to kill the monster bear. They knew when it attacked that it strode out of the water on its hind legs, its forearms raised. Under each arm was a small bald spot and they thought a sharp weapon might pierce its skin there.

The brothers dug a trench by the side of the lake and sharpened their axes. Then they hid in the trench and asked their sister's friends to lure the bear with a dance. When it rose from the lake in anger, the dancers shot arrows, but the points did not break its skin. As the bear roared past the hiding brothers, they jumped out and each hurled an axe under its arms. The bear staggered and fell. The brothers jumped on it and drove another axe into its forehead, killing it.

The brothers carried the bearskin back to their father. Many arrows dangled from its golden brown fur, but the father left them there. They were a constant reminder to the people that although the monster bear died, it was at great cost. If the young men and women had been respectful and not wasted the trout, many would still be alive and so would the magnificent bear.

15

REFUSE, REDUCE, OR REUSE: FIRST STEPS IN CUTTING WASTE

Refuse! Learning to Say "No!"

Go to your favorite store and pick out an item within your budget. It could be a box of individually wrapped fruit bars in three or four delicious flavors, complete with tradable stickers; a plastic sealed computer game that comes in DVD and CD formats, with instructions in fourteen languages; or a pair of wraparound running shoes that not only glow in the dark, but also jump (add a cool matching hat for as low as $20.00, with a scratch-and-win voucher). Before you even think of thwacking money down on the counter, rewind your mind and ask, "Do I really need this stuff?"

If you felt good about rejecting the snack, game, and shoes, you have successfully pre-cycled. That means you've looked, thought, and not bought. You considered both the product and the packaging and said no!

Refusing is more than pre-cycling. It is an attitude about "stuff" and makes you responsible for what you buy and what you throw away. Ask yourself these ten questions before making any individual, school, or family purchase and meet the challenge of pre-cycling – refusing wasteful stuff. You can personally reduce the amount of garbage created in your own community.

1. Do I really need this?
2. Will this last a long time?
3. Is this available in bulk?
4. Can this be repaired if it breaks?
5. When I am finished with this, can it be reused?

6. Is this made from recycled or biodegradable materials?
7. Can this be recycled when I'm finished with it?
8. Does this product come with as little packaging as possible?
9. Is there anything toxic or hazardous about this product or its packaging?
10. Was this product made responsibly?

THIS LIST NEEDS A NUMBER **ELEVEN**. "DO I REALLY, REALLY NEED THIS?"

Reduce: Trim Your Wasteline

What kind of creature sets waste goals, is in incredible waste shape, and regularly breaks its personal waste best? A Waste Olympian (W.O.). W.O.'s are pure gold for any community. Both individual and team players, they lead by example. And, they know that zero waste is the top score. Reaching that high standard starts with reducing.

Reducing is more important than recycling. With reducing, less is consumed; less is needed; and less waste is created in the first place. And each person's contribution counts. If you exercise your power to choose less, you too can be a W.O.

In the Bag

Will that be paper or plastic? How about neither? If every New Yorker used one less grocery bag each week all year long, five million pounds of waste would be kept out of landfill. What goes in the bag is equally important for every W.O. Buying loose will further reduce – choose your own fruit, veggies, candies, baked goods, and avoid packaged stuff.

In Ireland, grocery stores now charge about fifteen cents for each throwaway bag, resulting in a 90% decrease in the use of disposable bags. You can buy a reusable bag made from recycled plastic for about one euro (less than two dollars). When the bag wears out, the store replaces it for free and recycles it again.

W.O.'s use clean refillable mugs and water bottles too.

Paper-less

Reduce useless waste of trees and your personal paper waste by making a NO JUNK MAIL sign for your mailbox. Then contact the direct marketing association in your area and ask how you can be removed from bulk mailings you don't want or need.

If you have Internet access, ask for online school newsletters and sports notices. You can read your soccer schedule on the monitor, then write your schedule on a calendar without printing a page. When you do need paper, use both sides of every sheet – even computer paper.

w.o.'s save more trees by using cloth – rewashable rags – for messes and cleanups. Limit your use of paper towels, and only use paper products made from recycled paper.

World Record Holders

European countries have made packaging the responsibility of the manufacturers and the consumer. In Ireland, garbage bags are sold in a tight roll – no box, plastic bag, or twist ties. The bar-code and company name appear on a small sticker that holds the roll of bags tightly together. So the waste, beyond the garbage placed inside the bags, is tiny. That record is hard to beat!

Pass It On

One of the most popular summer Olympic events is the relay – one runner passes a baton to the next, each doing their bit to help the team reach the finish line. w.o.'s pass on in two ways. They give away "stuff" they no longer need, and, more importantly, they pass on their enthusiasm for reducing waste to the people around them. Encourage your family, friends, classmates, and neighbors to reduce too, and tell them to pass it on.

Reuse: Waste Not, Want Not

Do you have a grandmother who saves everything – from bits of string, aluminum foil, margarine tubs, milk bags, to old hats? Chances are, she grew up in the Depression or during the war years. "Waste not, want not" meant that nothing was ever thrown out if it could be reused. And, individuals were inventive in making do and extending the wear of essential everyday items.

During the 1930s, Millie Gourlay, a dietitian turned housewife, kept a trim home without a vacuum. A broom, a duster, and what she called elbow grease were her tools. To make her corn broom last longer, she cut the reinforced top off a worn-out nylon stocking and slid it up the brush end of the broom. This kept the bristles from splaying and breaking off.

AS MILLIE WOULD SAY, "A PENNY SAVED IS A PENNY EARNED."

Sadie Barnett raised seven children in the 1920s and '30s on the meager salary of her parson husband. Her unique cooking pots looked like a puzzle. Three wedge-shaped pots attached together, forming a circle, so she could cook a meal on one stove element, using less electricity. Later, she trimmed the braids and ponytails of her granddaughters with ribbons reclaimed from funeral flowers.

BRILLIANT IDEAS!

SADIE USED TO SAY, "COUNT YOUR **PENNIES** AND THE **DOLLARS** WILL LOOK AFTER THEMSELVES."

Henry, Sadie's third child, remembers the repairs required to keep seven kids in clothes. Worn collars and cuffs were removed, reversed, and sewn back on. With a lightbulb shoved inside, socks were darned with wool until the original color of the sock was no longer visible. Shirts and trousers had gussets (inserts in a seam) added to increase the size of the garment, accommodating fast-growing children. And, cardboard insoles kept Henry's feet dry when holes in his boots or galoshes allowed in rain or snow.

During the summer and fall of 1929, Harold Woollatt and millions of people worldwide invested all their savings in a fast-growing stock market. On a night in late October, Harold walked through the kitchen door and asked his wife, Madge, how much money she had in her wallet. It was $12.00. "That," said Harold, "is all the money we have in the world." Madge sold her 1928 Packard car and planted a Depression garden, replacing flowers with vegetables. And she worked with her husband to rebuild their lives. It remained game-on for Madge's son Charlie. No fancy hockey pads could be bought for him, so Charlie strapped magazines to his shins and played goal anyway.

21

Town kids were eager to trade with farm kids at lunchtime during the Depression years. Isabel Groh remembers taking a honey pail of food to school. Eggs, cheese, milk, and preserves were in good supply. But lunchroom trade was serious when meat was involved. Headcheese, a jellied and spiced loaf concocted from beef or pork, made nutritious use of all the leftover bits of an animal. Followed by a treat of bread, soaked in milk and sprinkled with sugar, meant satisfied, full tummies and an understanding of the expression "Waste not, want not."

Ruth Pitts, a wartime nursing student, had to look sharp for uniform inspection – the head nurse was a stickler for neatness. Stockings were in short supply and expensive, but Ruth's stocking mender saved her from many a tongue-lashing. Now, sixty years later, she still uses her mender for pantyhose repairs. Thrifty habits learned in her youth have reduced her life's footprint on Earth.

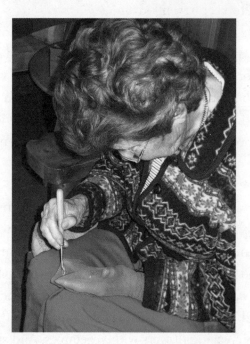

The *Apollo 13* Story

In April 1970, an almighty bang shook the Apollo 13 *spacecraft. Seconds later, the astronauts radioed Mission Control, "Houston, we have a problem." Flashing lights warned there was no oxygen in tank #2, while tank #1 was venting gas out into space. With two of three fuel cells out, Commander Jim Lovell and astronauts Jack Swigert and Fred Haise were no longer going to the Moon. They'd be lucky to get back to Earth alive – a distance of about 322,000 kilometers (200,000 miles).*

The astronauts' first reaction was disappointment. Aborting the mission meant failure. But what happened over the next four days was one of the most remarkable examples of reducing and reusing. As for refusing, they refused to give up.

A quick check of resources on the spaceship showed a damaged command module, a dying service module, and a lunar module meant to hold two people

for two days. The three astronauts had no choice but to crowd into the lunar module – a lifeboat about the size of two phone booths. They needed to conserve what little energy remained in order to point the spacecraft towards home. If they entered Earth's atmosphere at the wrong angle or too fast, they'd blow up or bounce off into space.

The astronauts turned off all nonessential machinery. The men nibbled on frozen hotdogs and drank juice in order to reduce the use of water. They stored urine in two plastic water bags and hoped they'd get home before they leaked. As the cabin temperature dropped to near freezing, the astronauts bundled up as best they could with no blankets on board.

Houston was ready for the next crisis. After two days, with three astronauts breathing in the lunar module, the carbon dioxide levels were dangerously high. The astronauts needed to reuse materials on the spaceship to modify a square filter from the command module to fit the lunar module's round filter hole. With no manuals or training procedures at their disposal, the ground personnel used cardboard, plastic bags, and adhesive tape – things that were also available on the spaceship – and designed a filter that fit "a square peg into a round hole." Houston radioed instructions to the astronauts, who put it together like a model. As Jim Lovell remembers, "… the contraption wasn't handsome, but it worked."

Two days later, *Apollo 13* splashed down into the Pacific Ocean close to the planned recovery spot. A resounding success for rocket science and refusing, reducing, and reusing!

RECYCLE: STEP IN THE RIGHT DIRECTION

A Symbol of Success

"Cool!" "Hip!" "Groovy." "Recycle." Some "in" words from thirty-five years ago are still popular today. In 1970, the North American recycling industry was young and needed a logo to identify what was recyclable. College student Gary Anderson entered a contest that offered a prize of $2500.00 to whomever designed the best symbol for recycling. Gary's winning entry was a modified Mobius loop – three arrows chasing each other around a triangle. August Ferdinand Möbius was a nineteenth-century mathematician and astronomer who saw the twisting, triangular loop as a continuous, one-sided, single-edged surface – whole, but with three distinct segments or planes. Over time, each segment has come to represent a step in recycling:

1. Collecting recyclable materials.
2. Manufacturing recycled goods.
3. Buying recycled products.

Plastics Don't Mix

In your neighborhood, you need to know what's recyclable. Even if the items are collected, adding unaccepted ones, such as those containing the wrong plastic resins, can ruin an entire batch, which will end up as garbage. Look on the bottom of plastic containers for a recycling symbol with a number from 1 to 7 stamped inside. Many communities recycle at least numbers 1 and 2.

In making just one thing, such as a side-view mirror holder for a car, there are bits and pieces of leftover plastic. The plastic has never been used (pre-consumer) and could be wasted. But roofing tiles can be made with pre-consumer plastic. That means leftovers from making car parts are remelted and made into tiles.

And More Symbols

Canada has developed an eco-logo of three doves that form the shape of a maple leaf. The doves represent government, industry, and consumers working together to protect the environment. Only environmentally safe products can display this symbol.

In Europe, consumers look for a green dot on packaging. Companies pay a fee to display the dot and the money is used to recycle packaging and invent packaging that's easy to recycle.

Watch for a Sustainable Forestry Certification (SFC) stamp on lumber and paper. This indicates the product has been made responsibly. When you choose these, you're guaranteed to make a smaller footprint.

Be a Label Reader

Label readers can reduce their footprints by choosing items that are made from recycled material. Buy throwaways, such as toilet paper, made from 100% post-consumer recycled paper. Post-consumer means the toilet paper was once a newspaper, or a cereal box, and not a freshly chopped tree.

Buying things made with recycled materials uses less energy. Oil and ore remain in the ground, trees are still standing, less goes to landfill, and the air is cleaner.

Recycled Plastic: The Possibilities Are Endless

Which of the following statements are true?

* Recycled peanut butter jars make dynamite basketball shoes.
* Plastic sleeves for storing hay or grain can be made into waterproof siding that won't crack.
* Shampoo bottles make tough mailboxes.
* Medical tubing can transform into mud flaps for a transport truck.
* Yogurt containers make terrific drainage pipes.
* Recycled dry cleaning bags make sturdy compost bins.
* Polyester fabric made from two plastic jugs can be sewn into one baseball hat.

If you answered true to all of the above, you're correct. In fact, you could be wearing a T-shirt made from pop bottles, or standing on carpet that was once take-out containers.

Plastic resin is made from oil – a precious nonrenewable resource. Invented in 1862, plastic has since become the most popular and widely used material in the United States. Recycling keeps tons of plastic out of landfill, where it takes up lots of room and, when buried deep, becomes worthless and takes centuries to break down. Every day, workers at material recycling facilities (MRF's) hand sort millions of plastic items collected through recycling programs. They know their plastic. Do you know yours?

The number stamped in the recycling symbol identifies the kind of plastic. In communities committed to plastics recycling, half of all plastics marked with a number 1 or 2 symbol is recovered and recycled, while less than six percent of numbers 3 to 7 is recovered or recycled.

Number 1 is PET (polyethylene terephthalate), a high-quality plastic that's lightweight, clear, and perfect for food and drink packaging. For example, all plastic pop bottles are made from PET. When PET is recycled, the labels and glue are washed off first. Then the containers are chopped into chips, rinsed, dried, and processed in a special generator. The final product is a plastic resin that looks almost exactly like resin made from oil. Recycled PET resin can be used again for items such as tennis ball fuzz, furniture, and surfboards.

Number 2 stands for HDPE (high-density polyethylene). Containers made from HDPE are stiffer and stronger, crafted to hold liquids such as milk, engine oil, or detergent. HDPE containers are not always washed before recycling, but are tossed right into a machine that melts and mixes all colors and kinds of containers together. Among other things, the liquid resin can be molded into bulletproof vests and plastic lumber that looks just like wood.

Number 3 or V (polyvinyl chloride) contains vinyl that weatherproofs such things as pigpens and traffic speed bumps.

Number 4 or LDPE (low-density polyethylene) is flexible enough for screw tops and squeeze bottles, but is also widely used in the manufacturing of plastic film and grocery bags.

Number 5 or pp (polypropylene) can handle syrups and hot liquids and is commonly used in tubs and lids for yogurt, margarine, ice cream, and shampoo bottles.

Number 6 or PS (polystyrene) is foamed for making meat trays, toys, and egg cartons.

Number 7 or OTHER is a mixture of plastics that's difficult to recycle.

Next time you take the recycling to the curb, count the number of number 1 PET bottles in the box. If there are five, that's the amount needed to make the fiberfill for your next winter coat!

Paper Weight

When you're in the park, put your arms around a tree. Give it a hug. It's hard, bumpy, and strong. Look up the trunk. Are there any birds or squirrels up there? Are you cool in the shade, protected from wind? Look around and try to find eleven other fully-grown trees. You and your family will use twelve trees' worth of paper over the next year. Promise those trees in the park that you'll do your part to recycle paper and buy recycled paper, so that fewer trees will need to be cut down.

If you live in a big city, chances are recycled paper is collected from your neighborhood, bought by a local paper packer, sold to a product producer, and sold back to you at a store. The more paper that's recycled the better because paper, like plastic, takes up a lot of space in landfill, but it's easy to recycle and is in high demand.

Paper collected for recycling is a commodity, just like corn or iron ore. Prices vary depending on the demand – how much is wanted – and the supply – how much is available. When the price is high, sometimes paper is stolen from curbside recycling boxes and sold illegally. Or bales of paper have heavy items stashed inside, such as bowling balls or car engines. The added weight raises the price, slows down the process, and ruins 300-million-dollar paper-making machines.

Paper manufacturing plants are often in production twenty-four hours a day. They use lots of recycled paper and need tons to keep the mills running. They buy baled paper from local recyclers as well as shredded paper from businesses. Both sources have passed through human hands and are called post-consumer recycled paper. Trimmings and rejected print from books and magazines are called pre-consumer recycled paper, meaning people have never used them. Both sources are kept out of landfill and end up in recycled paper products.

Weighty Facts about Paper Recycling

* Every ton of recycled paper saves seventeen trees, uses less than half the energy, half the water, creates one quarter of the air pollution, and employs five times the number of people than paper made from virgin wood pulp.
* Americans open only a quarter of the 4 million tons of junk mail they receive each year.
* One tree can remove up to 27 kg (59 lbs.) of air pollution each year.
* More paper is being recycled, but more is being used, too. Just because we are recycling more doesn't mean we are cutting down fewer trees. The amount going to landfill is going up, not down.

Lighten Up:
Weighing in on Packaging

When you buy something, it's a package deal. You want sauce on your spaghetti; it comes in a bottle. You want pop; it comes in a can. As a footprint-conscious consumer, you know that the empty container is yours too. So, you need to be aware of the costs involved in making and recycling different kinds of packages. And you can bet that weight is a huge cost factor. That means if you lighten up, you'll reduce your footprint.

Glass

Glass can be recycled indefinitely, but, at the same time, it's the heaviest and least valuable recyclable product. Making new glass from crushed glass uses half the energy required to manufacture glass from raw materials. And without mining and transporting sand and limestone, there's less pollution of water and air.

THE ENERGY SAVED BY *RECYCLING* ONE **GLASS BOTTLE** WILL KEEP A BULB LIKE ME SHINING FOR **FOUR** HOURS.

Recycled glass is a key ingredient in fiberglass insulation, sewer pipes, grit in chicken feed, and asphalt. But, the energy needed to recycle glass is higher than for plastic or aluminum. That's heavy stuff.

TEN TIMES MORE ENERGY? THAT'S A TWIST. FOR HUGE SAVINGS, *REPLACE* OLD LIGHT BULBS WITH COMPACT FLUORESCENT LIGHTING (CFL) BULBS LIKE ME.

4 HRS

Aluminum Cans

A tractor-trailer filled with squished aluminum cans sells its load for as much as $35,000.00. Aluminum cans are recycled over and over again and, in just six weeks, an empty can is recycled, remade, refilled, and transported back to a store shelf. Aluminum cans weigh less today than ever before, making them a light choice.

RECYCLING ONE **CAN** SAVES ENOUGH ENERGY FOR **THREE** HOURS OF TV.

Eleven-year-old Kathleen is in charge of her family's recycling and she takes her job seriously. Where she lives, in Black Tickle, Labrador, there's no municipal program. But once a year she sells cans and bottles that get shipped by barge to a recycling company in Newfoundland. Last year she made $60.00. Not bad spending money for a small amount of sorting.

Package Perfect

Look into my crystal ball. I see good things in small packages. I see feather-weight and totally recyclable containers. But hold on, my crystal ball is getting cloudy. *Ack!* It's turning orange! Is this possible? Can this be the perfect package?

In Nature, an orange comes well wrapped. The skin is thick and strong enough to protect the fruit inside, keeping it moist and ready to eat. It peels away easily, convenient for today's busy lifestyle. And the package biodegrades, returning goodness to Earth.

Some say that the best people-made container is an aseptic package. It is sanitary, lightweight, flexible, and designed for both what goes inside and you, the consumer. It can fit in a small hand for a single serving of juice, or stack in family sizes. And, where recycling facilities exist, this box can be completely recycled. Peeling apart an aseptic package shows how.

Layers of paper, plastic, and aluminum go into every pack. On the downside, the paper layer comes from live forests. But it's high-quality fiber, suitable for paper recycling. Recycled packs end up as paper towels, facial tissues, serviettes, and so on.

The outside and inside layers of the pack are thin HDPE (number 2) plastic. These layers seal out air and light while keeping the drink safely inside. One more plastic layer holds a barrier of aluminum foil – thinner than a human hair – in place. The foil is an energy saver, making it possible to store the juice without refrigeration. The plastic and foil easily separate from the paper and can be recycled. Unfortunately, few places actually recover and recycle the plastic and foil.

A single transport truck can deliver one million tightly rolled empty aseptic packages. One million empty cans or bottles need twenty trucks. Once filled, aseptic packs stack more tightly together than bottles or cans. Conserving space and weighing less saves delivery fuel and reduces greenhouse gases.

WILL WE EVER MAKE A PACKAGE AS PERFECT AS AN *ORANGE?*

FIRST WE HAVE TO INVENT A PACKAGE THAT'S MADE FROM 100% *RECYCLED* MATERIALS AND IS 100% *RECYCLABLE* ITSELF.

Not So Rotten Waste:
Toronto's Green Bin Program

Leftover pizza, pet litter, eggshells, and a dirty paper cup fed into a massive digesting machine will soon be nourishing a garden. Is this science fiction or a disgusting joke? Neither! The Green Bin Program has been adopted in cities all over the world. And if your community hasn't got one, why doesn't it?

In Toronto, the green bin has taken its place in the curbside lineup. In its first week, one family cut their sacked garbage from two large bags down to a single grocery bag. All that went to landfill was dryer lint, hair, nonrecyclable plastic, and the platter that broke at Thanksgiving. If every family pitches in with equal gusto, Toronto expects that by 2006, at least 60% of all household garbage will be kept out of landfill and turned into a useable commodity – recyclables and compost.

Most garbage belongs in a bin – blue, gray, garden compost, or green. For the green bin, there are two containers – one large outdoor bin on wheels and a small container for inside. To cut down on smells and the "yuck factor," a plastic grocery bag can be used to line the indoor container. Filled bags go in the outdoor bin and are wheeled to the curb each garbage day. Garbage collectors pick up the "green" separately from other garbage and take it to the nearest organics processing facility.

The entire jumble of soggy goop, plus lots of water, is tossed into a giant mixer called a hydropulper. Stirring breaks open the bags and added water makes it possible for any heavy unwanted things to sink and be removed through a valve. Lighter items, such as plastic bags, float to the surface, are raked off, and sent to landfill. The remaining garbage is spun, churned, squished, and divided into slurry (wet, syrupy garbage) and waste

36

(hard bits that won't break apart). Slurry is piped into a tall silo or tank called a digester, where it bubbles and percolates for two weeks. Methane gas is burned off to prevent explosions, but in future will be used to generate electricity. The slurry is squeezed through a corkscrew and forms a "cake," ready to compost. At a composting facility the cakes are aired, turned, and aged, until they look and smell like garden-ready compost.

In the past, garbage was low on many people's radar screens, but in this new millennium, it's everyone's responsibility. Toronto's Green Bin Program reduces the environmental footprint of the community and makes people deal with their own trash.

How Happiness Came — A Saami Story

The Saami people of Scandinavia tell the story of Akinidi, teaching their children that the natural world can bring more happiness than wealth and belongings.

From high in the sky, Akinidi, the daughter of the Sun, watched over life on Earth. Her job was to make all creatures happy. She had great success with caribou, birds, and even fish. But people were beyond her powers. Sometimes they laughed and were kind; other times they were grumpy and mean. Some people lived and dressed well, while many were hungry and poor. Bewildered by these strange creatures, Akinidi asked her father if she could go to Earth and live amongst them. She was sure she could bring happiness to everyone. Her father wondered why she'd give up living with the wind, clouds, and endless sky. However, after much pleading, he agreed to send her.

The next day Akinidi awoke, snuggled in reindeer skins. An elderly Saami couple peered down into her face, astonished at finding a beautiful girl, with sky blue eyes, in their childless home. "Can I live here as your daughter?" asked Akinidi. Speechless, the couple nodded *yes*.

As Akinidi explored her new home, she realized she was confined to a small island in the middle of a vast lake. The neighbors were pine trees, not people. Her father was pleased with himself – his daughter was safe and comfortable, with kind and loving company. But Akinidi wondered how she could make everyone happy from such a remote place. The couple kept her to themselves, saying she could visit other people when she fit into a maiden's dress.

Each day Akinidi cooked, cleaned, and mended fishing nets. In the evenings, she watched patiently as the old woman sewed her maiden's dress. Akinidi decorated the finished dress with small natural treasures she'd found on the island. The old woman marveled as the dress transformed into an exquisite gown, with pebbles and berries shining like jewels in Akinidi's intricate patterns. Finally, when the gown fit, the old man placed a crown of juniper sprigs on Akinidi's head. She ran to the shore and looked at her reflection in the lake. She was no longer a girl – she was a young woman.

The next day Akinidi packed a leather satchel and the old man took her to a Saami camp on the mainland. As Akinidi turned back the door flap of the closest tent and stepped inside, the family forgot their meal and stared in amazement at her radiant beauty. Each member touched her gown, hair, and cheeks. Akinidi took the smallest child's hand and led all the Saami down to the shore. One by one, they began singing and dancing, entranced by Akinidi's voice and graceful body. Never before had these people felt such joy. When they could dance no longer, Akinidi took berries and stones from her satchel, laid them on the ground, and covered them with her hands. "What's under here?" she asked, laughing. Everyone watched as she lifted her hands, revealing intricate designs from Nature – sunbeams, ptarmigan feathers, cloudberries – all sparkling like jewels. She scattered more stones and berries and challenged, "Make your own designs!"

Akinidi turned each person's designs into glistening jewels when they were sewn onto boots or coats. The camp bustled with activity and hummed with song. And, each night, Akinidi and her new friends danced until bedtime. But the elders were not impressed with all the singing, dancing, and pattern-making. They wanted handfuls of jewels. Jewels they could trade for reindeer, furs, and fuel. They ripped the jewels out of Akinidi's patterns and demanded more. Soon, their tents filled with furs, food, and trinkets and still they wanted more. Finally Akinidi said, "No! No more. Don't you see that the joy of the people and the beauty of the patterns are more valuable than jewels?"

The elders scolded the Saami people – who was Akinidi and what was wrong with their old lives? When the singing, dancing, and sewing of patterns continued, they visited an evil witch. She loathed happy people and gave the elders a magic green stone that could kill Akinidi. The elders rushed inside Akinidi's tent and flung the stone at her chest. Akinidi's last song disappeared up the smoke hole of the tent and her body faded away. The people watched as she returned to the sky and were filled with a great sense of loss.

But the Sun told Akinidi that she'd done her job well and the Saami people would never forget her songs, dances, and beautiful designs. They continue to bring happiness to this day.

LANDFILL OR INCINERATOR: WATCH YOUR STEP

World-Class Dump

What you are about to read is based on a true story. Do not try this at home – you may not be so lucky. This student's name has been changed to avoid embarrassment.

Chris' major project is due on garbage day. An entire year's work rests in his hands. He sits at the breakfast table, admiring over fifty pages of text, illustrations, maps, and an annotated bibliography. The squeal of the garbage truck rouses him from his daydream and he whirls into action. The folded newspaper slips neatly into his backpack and his project flies into a garbage bag. *Zip up the backpack, tie up the bag, and rush out the door.* Chris drops the garbage bag into the waiting jaws of the big green truck, slings his backpack over his shoulder, and heads for the bus stop.

When Chris arrives at class, he opens his backpack and pulls out the daily news. Where's the slick blue folder he held at breakfast?

The truck driver, meanwhile, steers into an enormous industrial site, rolls up to the weigh scales, and waves at the attendant. A swirl of dust, a few circling vultures, and a whiff of fresh garbage are clues that this is one of North America's largest landfills. Buried in the truck's belly, amongst hundreds of other garbage bags, is Chris' project.

This landfill site is as good as it gets. A natural lining of clay goes down 80 meters (262 feet) from the surface, sealing garbage in. Tall portable screens trap airborne litter, while a perimeter of mounded-up soil and the surrounding cornfields help keep garbage out of the neighbors' view.

The business of operating a landfill requires making space ready to receive loads of trash. Enormous earth-moving machines dig a "cell" or pit, then giant dump trucks remove the soil and stock-pile it for later use. Drains and pipes are installed in the bottom to trap runoff liquid called leachate and to suck off methane gas. Recycled woodchips, a layer of stones, and a fabric liner made from geo-textile material protect the bottom of each cell.

Over a hundred loads of garbage arrive at this dump every working day. Some trucks tip their loads; others have a "walking floor" that moves the garbage out the back of the truck. All garbage is deposited at the "tipping face" – the part of the cell that's being filled. Chris' bag falls to the top of a mound and moments later is squished flat by "Rex" – a mean-looking truck called a crusher.

Every evening a layer of soil or woodchips is spread over the garbage to cover the smell and deter scavengers, such as rodents, coyotes, and wild birds. This layer is removed each morning so that as much garbage as possible can be crammed into each cell. With the garbage exposed once again to the air, birds are discouraged from daytime feeding by trained hunting falcons and loud blasts from a pyrotechnics gun. Birds at a landfill can spread litter and disease.

The landfill acts as a large filter. Liquids from the garbage seep through the trash, ending up as leachate in the bottom. Leachate can contain household hazardous waste – such as cleaners, batteries, drugs, or paint – that's toxic to both people and the environment. This sewagelike brew is pumped from the cell to an on-site water purification plant.

Leachate is treated through many steps, including the removal of solids, bits of nonorganic garbage, and organic matter. Solids are buried in the landfill and, when the remaining liquid is considered safe, it is discharged into the local creek.

A by-product of rotting garbage is methane gas. At this landfill, methane is vacuumed into a huge storage cylinder and burned off – energy up in smoke. Methane is a greenhouse gas that changes to a less powerful greenhouse gas when it is burned. Communities are beginning to divert methane into an engine ten times the size of a large car, run it through a generator, and add the resulting electricity to the local supply system or "grid." This process produces green energy from garbage people have thrown away.

When Chris gets home from school, he realizes his dreadful mistake and calls the landfill site. Lucky for him, the workers are able to locate the area where garbage from his neighborhood was dumped. His project is retrieved – smellier and flatter than before, but in one piece.

THAT'S PROBABLY THE STRANGEST EXCUSE HIS TEACHER EVER HEARD.

CAREFUL SORTING AND RECYCLING AT HOME KEEPS UNWANTED GARBABE OUT OF LANDFILL.

Garbology

In landfills, there is no such thing as good garbage. If it's stuffed in a bag, it doesn't matter if it's potato peelings or plastic wrap. The bags are squished tight by machines and other garbage, so there is virtually no air, sunlight, or moisture – the necessary ingredients for decomposition. All in together, today's household garbage becomes part of an ever-growing layer cake that takes years, centuries, even millennia, to rot.

Garbologists study household garbage. Like archaeologists or geologists, they drill landfills for core samples and examine the layers. Packed between newspapers, hotdogs, diapers, and spinach salad are condensed insights into how people live. Garbologists know what we eat, use, and waste.

William Rathje has dug deep into North American landfills for over thirty years and knows who wastes what. His studies show that people lie about what's in their garbage. Most families won't admit it, but 15% of food spoils before it's eaten; people drink more pop and eat fewer vegetables than they claim. And while more paper is being recycled, there are more magazines, newspapers, flyers, throwaways, and paper packages than ever before. Almost half the waste arriving at landfills is paper. Rathje tracked the garbage habits of ordinary people and found that as many recyclables end up in the trash as in the recycling bin. Some people are meticulous about sorting cans and bottles, but then throw hazardous waste, such as batteries, straight into the garbage.

Mongo hunters (people who salvage garbage from streets and trash heaps) and dumpster divers are "garbage guerrillas," mining trash for anything they can turn into cash. In big cities such as New York, self-employed recyclers know where and when to find good

44

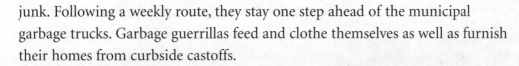

junk. Following a weekly route, they stay one step ahead of the municipal garbage trucks. Garbage guerrillas feed and clothe themselves as well as furnish their homes from curbside castoffs.

Even in remote parts of the world, wild scavengers track down useable garbage. Polar bears can smell a meal over a mile away. When the ice thins in spring and seals can't be caught, some bears follow their noses to the closest dump. Patient hunters, they wait for fresh garbage deliveries or rip open bags, looking for fatty food. Unfortunately, bears aren't picky eaters and can die from eating the can along with the sardines, or drinking motor oil. And bears hooked on garbage often end up shot, or tranquilized and relocated for aggressive behavior towards people – the makers of the garbage.

Garbologists, mongo hunters, and polar bears would all agree that people throw out lots of good stuff. But only garbologists would say the key to solving landfill problems is buying and using less.

NIMBY — Not In *My* Backyard!

No one wants to be neighbors with anything (or anyone) yucky. If a traditional garbage dump were a living creature, it would be described as gaseous, smelly, smoky, messy, and downright rotten. Would it make a good neighbor? Silly question. No fence would be high enough, no air freshener strong enough to keep it from invading your space. Is it any wonder that people have adopted the NIMBY (not in my backyard) attitude towards garbage disposal? Garbage usually stinks, attracts scavengers, travels in noisy trucks, and can pollute groundwater. On the other hand, people produce garbage and need places to stash their trash. Like it or not, landfills are part of every community, but some make better neighbors than others.

If you live in Vancouver, Burns Bog – the largest domed peat bog in North America – is in your backyard. One corner of the bog is home to the largest operating landfill in Canada. Since it opened in 1966, there has been a struggle between two groups – the developers and the "boggites." The first group sees the land's potential – beyond landfilling – to include a possible golf course, shopping mall, racetrack, farms, and so on; the boggites value the area for being a natural reserve, home to many fragile and unique species.

Bogs are composed of sphagnum moss and form less than 3% of Earth's surface. But they store three times the amount of carbon as tropical rainforests. Not only is

Burns Bog an important carbon storehouse, it also filters the air, releases valuable oxygen, and reduces local flooding. It actively combats climate change and

removes pollutants from the Fraser River Delta. Burns Bog is a sensitive ecosystem, with highly acidic soil. It takes years for fallen trees to rot in it, and creatures that die naturally become mummified. Even footprints left on the surface last for months, or years. At the same time, Burns Bog is rich with nearly three hundred rare, unusual, and common wildlife species. In one visit you could see a sunshine yellow skunk cabbage; a beaver constructing a dam that will help keep water levels high; a black bear fishing for its supper; a flock of sandhill cranes resting and feeding before flying south for the winter.

The Vancouver Landfill and Burns Bog are stuck with each other.

The landfill has room for fifty more years' worth of garbage. As of March 2004, fifty thousand acres of the bog is a legally protected ecosystem. Local and provincial governments purchased the land and have planned for the future of the bog. They will not consider any further development plans so that wildlife will continue to roam and human visitors can explore the wonders of Burns Bog – as long as they walk on the boardwalks and leave no footprints.

Wastes of Time

If you don't want a dump in your backyard, you probably wouldn't want to live in a house made of kitchen waste, but people have over time.

Orkney Islands, Scotland: 3000 B.C.

Five thousand years ago, that's just what the people of Skara Brae did. In fact, they constructed most of the walls in their prehistoric village out of claylike material, called midden, created by rotting vegetable matter, bones, and animal dung mixed in with empty shells, ash, stones, and broken pottery.

Archaeologists think the Neolithic villagers deliberately threw all their waste in one place until it formed midden. They carried it to their building site, piled it into mounds, and then dug down into the midden to make rooms and hallways. Finally, they lined the inside walls of their partly underground village with flagstone.

Why midden? The material was available, strong as well as weatherproof. They could shape their living spaces and connect them with snaking entrance passageways that kept out cold winds and stray animals. And once their garbage changed from waste to midden, it didn't smell anymore.

Atlantic Seacoast: 4500 B.C.

Archaeologists learn a lot about prehistoric humans by digging into refuse heaps, also called middens. Ancient people who lived on the coasts of both Europe and North America left huge shell middens near where they harvested oysters, clams, mussels, limpets, cockles, and other shellfish. They must have returned year after year for many generations because some of these middens are larger than football fields and several meters deep. By studying the contents of middens, scientists not only learn what shellfish, fish, and other animals prehistoric people ate, but also the tools and weapons they used to gather food. In some cases, the shape of the midden shows whether people sat in a crescent or a circle at mealtime.

Perhaps strangest of all, scientists have found burials in middens. These are not bodies thrown on a trash heap – they are often burials in which people are carefully laid out with their personal treasures, including necklaces and hunting spears. Some archaeologists think middens, which families returned to over and over again in life, gave ancient people a feeling of community.

Fire, Fuel, and Fumes: Case Study of a Modern Energy-From-Waste (EFW) Incinerator

Some people think that incinerators are unfit for human garbage consumption. They burn everything they're fed and their diet is noxious. Smoke and fumes contribute to climate change and fall back to Earth as acid rain. And the waste ash requires a special landfill. Many communities have banned incinerators, but now some are reconsidering. The high cost of property for landfills and the NIMBY approach to garbage, combined with cleaner incineration technology from Europe, make this waste treatment an option.

In Peel Region, Ontario, about one million people recycle nearly half their waste through recycling programs and send the rest to an energy-from-waste facility. In a typical facility, over 500 metric tons (550 tons) of nonhazardous solid waste arrive every weekday as trucks continually weigh in, dump their load, and weigh out. A monstrous machine, fitted with a handlike claw, sifts and squeezes the garbage bags, looking for large metal items, such as bikes, which are removed and recycled. The garbage is processed in a seven-day cycle in order to produce a steady flow of fuel and avoid fires. If the garbage is left in a pile for a day or two, the rotting process causes methane gas to build up and it can burst into flames.

Garbage is loaded into a receptacle called a hopper and pushed through the incinerator's fire door into a giant oven. When the garbage catches fire, the incinerator makes steam that rotates a turbine. The turbine runs a generator that produces electricity. Right outside the plant, the electricity feeds into the local grid, providing power to six thousand homes.

Ash and fumes are the end products of incineration. Ash left at the bottom of the incinerator is called bottom ash. Metals taken from bottom ash are recycled or landfilled. The remaining ash is cooled with water and drained. This material may be sold as filler for landfills if it passes a toxicity test. It's also tested as an ingredient in asphalt. The incinerator operators say the ash is safe enough to be handled, but a small amount goes to a toxic waste site.

So, what goes up the smokestack? Smoke and fumes from inside the incinerator are cooled, made acid-neutral, and passed through two hundred and forty filter bags. The ash in the bags is called fly ash and is treated as hazardous waste. The air above the smokestack appears clear and meets all government standards. With careful monitoring and testing of the air quality, can we breathe a sigh of relief?

Hazardous Waste: Keep Out!

Take a good look around. Can you identify anything you'd consider hazardous or toxic? Not the dog's breakfast; but plant food, a handheld computer game, car tires, or an antique model boat. Hiding inside quite ordinary things are dioxins, asbestos, mercury, or lead. Left intact and undisturbed they pose little threat, but thrown out or burned up they can suddenly become dangerous. Hazardous waste must be disposed of properly to keep the air, ground, and water safe.

There are some waste cargoes that won't go away, as told in the bizarre and scary saga of the *Khian Sea*. In 1984, news leaked out that ash delivered from Philadelphia's incinerator to a New Jersey landfill was hazardous waste. New Jersey declared, "Keep out!" Philadelphia decided to take its ash elsewhere and, in September 1986, loaded up a cargo ship called the *Khian Sea*. When she reached the Bahamas, she was refused entry. Next stop, Dominican Republic. *Forget it!* Honduras, Panama, Bermuda. *No way.* The unwanted cargo ship headed across the Atlantic to Guinea-Bissau and then to the Netherlands Antilles – a long way for nothing. Finally, fourteen months later, the Haitian government agreed to accept the *Khian Sea*'s cargo, described as "fertilizer." It was so "safe," one crewman supposedly ate a mouthful of ash. But the environmental group Greenpeace alerted Haiti that the ship was, in fact, full of toxic waste. While the Haitians were canceling the *Khian Sea*'s permit, the crew dumped 3,628 metric tons (4,000 tons) of ash on a beach and slunk off into the dark. Over the next ten months, the ship changed names twice, attempting to disguise its true identity. After trying to offload the rest of the ash in eleven different countries, the ship's cargo vanished

> BATTERIES ARE INCLUDED – AS TOXIC WASTE.

somewhere between Singapore and Sri Lanka – probably tossed overboard.

Four years later, in 1990, five hundred mysterious envelopes came by mail to the offices of Philadelphia's mayor and the U.S. Environmental Protection Agency. The envelopes read, "Contains Philadelphia Waste. Return to Sender." There was no return address. While the Pacific Ocean could only swallow up the toxic ash, the Haitians protested.

Philadelphia was eventually forced to contribute to the cleanup cost and, by April 2000, all of the ash was removed from Haiti for permanent storage in the United States.

HAITI THINKS POLLUTERS SHOULD CLEAN UP THEIR OWN MESSES. WHAT DO YOU THINK?

LITTERING AND DUMPING: STEPPING OUT OF LINE

Litter Is an Attitude

The fabled Inca Trail to Machu Picchu in Peru, the icy final ascent up Mount Everest in Nepal, and your local bus stop – what do they have in common? Litter. Yes, litter. This dirty human habit now soils even the wildest and most remote corners of our planet.

The Inca Trail

The Inca Trail starts near Cuzco, the ancient capital city of the Incas in the Andes

Mountains of South America. The trail winds through cloud forest, climbs up and down prehistoric staircases, and passes the ruins of Incan way stations and temples. After four days, hikers finally reach the magical Incan fortress of Machu Picchu. The trail and fortress are so steeped in history and beauty that the United Nations has named the

area a World Heritage Site. Every day, hundreds of tourists set out to hike the trail and, when they buy their permits, agree to carry out all garbage.

In July 2002, Kate and seven other students hiked the trail to collect what tourists left behind. Armed with garden gloves, white canvas sacks, and sticks, the students bagged 1,360 kg (2,992 lbs.) of garbage along the trail. Empty plastic water bottles made up a quarter of the litter. Kate and her friends had to stop collecting the used toilet paper they found because it made them sick. Shocked, Kate wondered, *Why can't people be bothered? Why leave any mark on the world? Every piece of litter counts and accumulates.*

Mount Everest

The litter on the trail from the last camp to the summit of Mount Everest is specialized – mostly empty oxygen bottles, discarded fuel canisters, ropes, and human remains. Climbers, struggling to survive howling winds, blizzards, narrow ice bridges, steep cliffs, and thin air, are often forced to abandon gear to get down to safety. The amount of litter is so great that people call Mount Everest the highest garbage dump in the world. And removing what's left near the summit is dangerous and often impossible.

Closer to Home

Some litter has "legs." Light and easily caught by wind or flowing water, a plastic grocery bag tossed in the ditch at a bus stop could end up floating in the ocean half a world away. Every year, thousands of sea turtles, seabirds, seals, and dolphins die, mistaking littered plastic bags for tasty jellyfish or squid.

PAPER LITTER DISAPPEARS THE FASTEST. A TISSUE STARTS BREAKING DOWN IN A COUPLE OF WEEKS, WHILE A PLASTIC BAG TAKES ONE THOUSAND YEARS TO FLAKE APART.

A POP CAN MIGHT TAKE THREE HUNDRED YEARS.

GLASS LASTS A LONG TIME – A MILLION YEARS FOR A BOTTLE!

Garbage in the Deepfreeze

As the spring sun warms the far northern landscape, a winter's worth of garbage, litter, and lost treasure appears through the melting snow. A yard cleanup in Yellowknife, Northwest Territories, might bag empty pop cans, soggy candy wrappers, and plastic bags as well as lost mittens, broken ski poles, axe handles, toboggans, and much more. When families have sorted out what they want to keep, they go "shopping." That's local slang for going to the dump. They drop off their garbage and then dig for stuff they might need – a bike tire, a fishing rod, a gas can, who knows? A local news reporter even writes about tales from the dump when shopping is unusually brisk.

Recycling is a challenge in the North. Towns are so far away from markets that shipping bales of newspapers or plastic bottles "outside" (what people from Alaska and Canada's northern territories call anywhere south) to recyclers is expensive. Even collecting enough newspapers to make a bale can be hard because communities are small. And composting, when most of the year is below freezing, seems impossible.

While going "shopping" can be fun, most garbage is not recovered. Dumps are a big waste of resources and they are not good for the environment. Dumps attract bears, and garbage bears are dangerous. Worse, dumps melt permafrost. Much of the ground in the Arctic is permanently frozen, sometimes to depths of hundreds of meters. In summer, only the top layer melts to support plant life. But a dump interferes with the top layer and can cause thawing below it, creating a wet, widening sinkhole – an especially nasty footprint. It's possible to construct landfills where the permafrost is insulated with deep gravel, but that's expensive.

Many Northerners want to protect their land and make recycling work. In Iqaluit, Nunavut, members of the Recycling Society are experimenting with composting food scraps under tarpaulins during the short summer. In Yukon, the deposit on drink containers is so high it pays to return bottles, cans, and drink boxes rather than toss them away. And, in keeping with the rule that it's best to reuse, the dump in Tagish, Yukon, has a corner called Tiffany's for people to leave items for others to take.

Still, it's incredible how much is thrown away. In a river gorge near Carcross, Yukon, Steve found and winched out the rusty body of a 1927 Model T Ford. The slogan *Carcross or Bust* was painted on the back of the wreck. Steve got it running with old engine parts and materials he found along the side of a road and in a junkyard at a local gas station. His friend Ian dug up an old canvas tent in the village dump to use for the convertible roof. The car ran so well, Steve drove it down the Alaska Highway, across Canada all the way to Nova Scotia. Then he rumbled back across the continent to South Dakota, where he finally sold it. Ian's friends in Yukon gave him the nickname "Raven" after the bird that regularly "shops" in northern dumps.

Space Junkyard

5 ... 4 ... 3 ... 2 ... 1 ...

The rocket carrying a communications satellite blasts off from its launch pad in Kazakhstan, Russia. The booster engines and fuel tanks driving the rocket's powerful thrust are soon used up and jettisoned from the spacecraft. But the satellite speeds on into orbit.

The spent engines and tanks crash to the ground under the rocket's flight path. Nearby villagers and farmers often scavenge the wreckage. They make shovels, sleds, and other equipment from the scavenged parts and the housing of old Soyuz spacecraft. But cancer is on the rise in the area and health workers blame the toxic chemicals in rocket fuel and salvage.

Meanwhile, in space, the satellite has to dodge derelict spaceships and other satellites that are breaking up, but still orbiting Earth. It's a moving junkyard up there – most of it traveling at nearly 30,000 kilometers an hour (18,600 mph). NASA routinely tracks the whereabouts and orbits of 11,000 pieces of debris greater than 10 cm (4 in.) in size. But there are tens of millions of smaller pieces that are harder to detect. In 1983, a fleck of paint chipped the windshield of the Space Shuttle *Challenger*. Fortunately, the crew was unharmed.

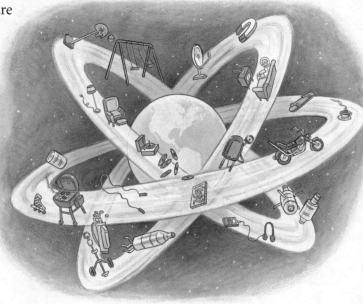

The International Space Station and the Space Shuttle are now made to withstand collisions with tiny bits of debris and to detect and maneuver away from much larger pieces of junk. They still remain at risk for collision with the 100,000 or so pieces in between.

Today, most spacecraft are programmed to return to Earth or burn up at the end of their missions, so they don't add to the orbiting junkyard. But with present technology, it's not possible to remove what's up there already. Depending on how high the orbit, it could take decades for junk in space to fall back to Earth.

Alien Invaders

Aliens are invading the Great Lakes! Sounds impossible, but it's true. Over 160 plants and animals, at home in other parts of the world, are successfully taking over. And some of these aliens were dumped into the lakes as living garbage.

Zebra Mussels

One of the most successful invaders is the zebra mussel, a shellfish from the Black and Caspian Sea regions of Asia. In 1988, zebra mussel larvae, invisible to the human eye and with no natural predators in North America, traveled across the Atlantic Ocean like stowaways in a freighter's ballast (water taken on board to stabilize the ship). When the freighter entered Lake St. Clair, the crew flushed out the ballast because it was no longer needed. The young mussels, drifting on currents, grew into adults. Then the adults attached themselves onto boat hulls, nets, buoys, and other floating debris and spread through all five Great Lakes in just ten years. Since each female mussel produces a million eggs a year, it wasn't long before billions of zebra mussels overran the lakes and nearby rivers.

Adult zebra mussels live in colonies and fasten to almost any hard surface underwater. If they cling to a native clam, they slowly kill it because the clam cannot move with that much weight on its shell. Lake St. Clair clams are now almost extinct. When zebra mussels attach to water-intake pipes, the colony soon plugs them. Munroe, Michigan, had no water for three days once because zebra mussels clogged the water intakes.

Power companies, steel manufacturers, city water utilities, even golf course owners, cumulatively spend hundreds of millions of dollars a year to keep zebra mussels out of their water pipes. And park officials spend time and money raking the sharp shells off beaches.

Hydrilla

Some aliens are poised to invade the Great Lakes, but haven't yet. Hydrilla is one. This aquarium plant, at home in Korea and India, was tossed into a Florida river with water from someone's fish tank in the late 1950s. Hydrilla is heading north and, in state after state, has carpeted the surface of ponds and lakes so that no light shines into the water. Fish, shellfish, and other plants die without light. Scientists are hoping to stop hydrilla's spread before it takes hold in the Great Lakes.

Just when new laws have stopped the uncontrolled dumping of garbage, raw sewage, and industrial waste, the Great Lakes now face invading species. Small thoughtless steps are growing into monster footprints in the largest reservoir of freshwater on Earth.

Nature's Cleanup Crew

Worms, fungi, bacteria, snails, and other decomposers are Nature's garbage workers. They filter, decontaminate, and clean waste, breaking it down and returning it to Earth for reuse. Without them, we could be knee-deep in waste; yet we ignore decomposers and take their essential services for granted. This story from Southeast Asia shows how even the grandest of creatures is subject to Nature's lowly waste workers. With just a little more respect for one decomposer, the story would have turned out differently.

The Snail, the Horse, and the Mango – A Burmese Folktale

One hot day, an old snail found a ripe mango lying on the side of the road. Suddenly an arrogant horse pranced up and neighed, "Stand back. That mango's for me."

"But I was here first," the old snail said. "Let me take one bite and I'll leave you the rest."

"No," the horse snorted, "I'm stronger, more important, and faster than you. I want to eat it before you smear it with your slime."

"You may be stronger and more important," the old snail replied, "but you are not faster. Let's have a race. The winner eats the mango."

The idea of a race against a snail was so ridiculous, the horse couldn't think of a reason to decline. "Fine," he whinnied, "but don't expect to win. I'm going to leave you in my dust."

"Since I'm the smallest, I'll set the rules," the old snail said. "Meet me at sunrise at the white temple, and we'll race back up the river road to this mango."

The horse agreed and, with a toss of his mane, galloped off.

A little wren had been listening from the treetop. "Snail, I want to see you win the race, but how can you? The temple is miles from here."

"I have a plan and you can help," said the old snail. "Fly around and ask my brothers, sisters, and cousins to meet me tonight at the gray rock on the river." The wren happily delivered the snail's message.

That night, by the river, the old snail whispered to a great assembly of snails, listening intently, nodding their antennae, and snuffling little snail laughs. Then, all the snails jumped into the

river, crawling out, one at a time, at each milestone along the road. The old snail crawled out last, at the white temple, just in time to meet the horse for the race.

The horse was amazed to see the snail at all.

"There's one rule," said the snail. "Since I am so small, you may confuse me for a rock, or clump of dirt. Whenever one of us reaches a milestone, call out to establish who is there first."

The horse agreed,
certain he would be
first at every milestone.

The wren chirped to start the race
and the horse trotted off, taking his time, well
ahead of the snail. When he got to the first milestone, the horse remembered the rule and
neighed.

Ahead on the road a snail called back,
"Too late, I got there first." The horse was amazed
and, without looking at the snail carefully, trotted on
a little faster.

At the next milestone, the horse called out again,
but ahead on the road
was a snail declaring, "Sorry, I got
there first again."

The horse couldn't believe
his ears and started to gallop.
But, at each milestone, the horse
found a snail already there.
The horse started racing faster
and faster, not stopping for a
drink even as the day grew
hotter and hotter. Finally he
collapsed and died before ever
reaching the mango.

And so the old snail and all its
relatives got to eat the mango.
They also ate the horse, until
there was nothing left but hard
white bones.

Sizing Your Footprint

Do you want to trim your footprint down to size? First, decide which shoe fits.

Way Too Big

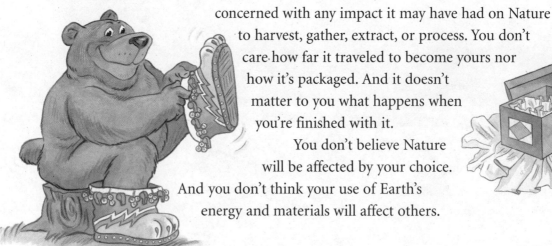

You buy an item because you want it, not because you need it. You aren't concerned with any impact it may have had on Nature to harvest, gather, extract, or process. You don't care how far it traveled to become yours nor how it's packaged. And it doesn't matter to you what happens when you're finished with it. You don't believe Nature will be affected by your choice. And you don't think your use of Earth's energy and materials will affect others.

Too Big

You may wonder if you need an item before you buy it, but you buy it anyway. You may notice what material it's made from, but not what it cost Nature to harvest, gather, or extract. You may see that your purchase is overpackaged, but you don't worry about that. You don't consider what water and energy were used for its manufacture and

transport, or will be needed when you use it. You'll wait until the time comes before you decide how to dispose of it.

You're aware of Nature and other people, but they don't affect your purchase.

Just Right

You buy an item only if you need it. You look for a brand made from reused or recycled material. If that's not available, you choose one made from a material that had little impact on Nature to gather, harvest, or extract. You consider if much energy or water was needed in its manufacture or will be needed when you use it. You look to see if it was produced locally and will not buy an item transported a great distance. You refuse any unnecessary packaging. Finally, you think about whether the item can be reused or recycled when you've finished with it, or at least disposed of with little impact on Nature.

You respect Nature and try to take only your fair share.

Too Small

Your family has trouble making ends meet. Getting good food, adequate shelter, and proper clothing is not always easy. You don't have a lot of choices and only a few treats.

Way Too Small

You go hungry some days and live in inadequate housing. Your clothing is limited and you may not own shoes that fit. You have few choices.

Making Choices

When you play hockey, you can measure your performance on the ice by tracking your plus-minus score. If your team scores while you're playing, you earn one point. If the other team scores, you lose one. Your plus-minus score is the total you earn in a game. The higher your score, the bigger part you played in the team's success.

Next time you buy something, you can calculate its environmental plus-minus score before making your choice. But this time, unlike hockey, you're trying to keep a low total. Use the following scorecard and see how your purchase affects Nature and your ecological footprint size. (If you want to measure it more accurately, try the calculator at *www.footprintnetwork.org*.)

Choose what you want to buy and then add up all the relevant pluses and minuses to come to a final total. See if it is greater or smaller than your own shoe size – in this game, that would be an acceptable score.

1. What material is your purchase made from?
    a. Plant (paper, wood, cotton, vegetable)   +2
    b. Animal (leather, meat, fur)   +3
    c. Mineral (metal, oil, plastic)   +5
    d. A mixture (of materials)   +8
    e. Secondhand   -4
    f. Certified organically grown   -2

    If you know that certified good forest practices were implemented or environmental safeguards used in extraction – beyond government regulation – give yourself a bonus of -2.

2. How was it made?
    a. By hand   0
    b. Using a small amount of energy and/or water   +2
    c. Using a moderate amount of energy and/or water   +5
    d. Using a significant amount of energy and/or water   +15

If you answered b, c, or d above, but notice that energy-efficient or water-saving procedures were applied, give yourself a bonus of -1.

3. How far did it travel?
   a. Carried on foot   0
   b. Locally produced (under 100 km or 62 mi.)   +2
   c. Produced outside your province or state   +3
   d. Imported   +10

If you answered b, c, or d above, but notice that energy-efficient fuel was used, add a bonus of -1.

ACK! **PLUS 10**, WHY SO MUCH?

COUGH, COUGH! TRANSPORT ADDS POLLUTION TO THE AIR — JUST FOR STARTERS.

4. How is it sold?
   a. No packaging or bulk   0
   b. Recyclable packaging   +1
   c. Nonrecyclable packaging   +2
   d. Excessive, wasteful packaging   +5

5. How is it used?
   a. No power, no pollution — 0
   b. Needs a little power/fuel to operate — +2
   c. Emits pollution (fumes, excessive noise) — +10
   d. Alters natural landscape — +15
   e. Operates with reusable batteries or energy-saving devices — -1

6. How is it maintained and cleaned?
   a. By hand — 0
   b. Needs a little fuel and/or water to maintain — +1
   c. Needs substantial fuel and/or water to maintain — +5
   d. By repairing or upgrading — -2

7. How can it be disposed of?
    a. Put into regular municipal garbage   +3
    b. Discarded outside proper waste disposal   +5
    c. Tossed in with items containing toxic chemical materials   +8
    d. Reused – sold or given away   -8
    e. Composted   -5
    f. Recycled   -3
    g. Taken to a household hazardous-waste depot
        for special handling and treatment, if toxic   -2

Why not measure the footprint of a purchase without going to the store?
Calculate and compare the plus-minus scores of a pair of imported, designer
running shoes that you throw into the regular garbage when you have out-
grown them to a pair of national-brand runners that you give to a charity.

Full Circle

Once you are committed to reducing your footprint, do you have to throw your garbage into the right container every time? Does pitching an apple core in with the bottles have anything to do with saving an endangered species, such as a tiger?

Consider, for a moment, the apple. Red, delicious, juicy, crisp – but actually not much more than water molecules and carbon atoms that have been around since the solar system formed about 4.5 billion years ago.

Any one of the carbon atoms in the apple could have been part of a rocky cliff, or a woolly mammoth's tusk, or a log in a campfire, or many other things before it became part of your apple. And one of the water molecules in the apple could have been part of a comet's tail, or a dinosaur's eye, or rain that fell a thousand different times.

Eat the apple. The carbon and water will become part of your hair, or muscle, or maybe, in this case, your skin. Yes, you are made up of billion-year-old parts.

Now, say a flake of skin rubs off into your sock, which is then laundered. The skin is washed down the drain. Your skin cell could end up in a lake and become part of a fish egg, or a duck, or a bulrush … all the connections between you and the apple now carry on into the future. Maybe for another 4.5 billion years.

But don't forget the core. If you throw that into the compost, the core's carbon and water will soon become part of a carrot, or a summer flower, or a fat raccoon – just imagine….

Or, if you throw it into the town garbage, the core may end up in the municipal landfill and could mummify for years. The carbon might eventually become methane gas and be used to heat a home. The water may collect as leachate, and once cleaned, return to Nature. If the core is incinerated, the carbon will likely end up as ash and the water will escape as a gas. Both will return to Nature over time.

And if you toss the core on the side of the road, it could become part of a crow, or a dandelion, or even a nasty toxic puddle.

You can return the goodness of the core back to Nature quickly. Or, you can send it down a longer route. Either way, you and the apple are fundamentally and powerfully connected.

You and everything in Nature are connected. It's a small world – you are one link in Nature's circle. And that includes animals like the magnificent but imperiled tiger. Every thoughtful effort you make to reduce your footprint is important to Nature, to animals, and to you.

We do not weave the web of life … we are just a strand in it. Whatever we do to the web … we do to ourselves. – Chief Seattle, 1854.

Glossary

biodegradable: made of materials that will break down harmlessly through natural processes

blue box: a container that holds dry recyclable household waste, such as tin cans, papers, plastic and glass bottles. The blue box is carried to the curbside for special pickup in many towns and cities. See *green bin, recycle.*

compost: a mixture of decayed food and garden waste used for fertilizer. See *organics.*

consume: use or use up materials or articles

decomposition: a natural form of recycling in which a material decays, breaks down, and returns to the environment

ecological footprint: a measure of the mark we leave on the natural world. It considers how much land and sea are required to provide us with the water, energy, and food we need to support our lifestyles. It helps us judge whether we are overusing the natural environment, or whether we are leaving enough for Nature to recover each year to fulfill our needs again.

environment: the air, water, climate, rocks, soil, wildlife, and all other surroundings that affect the lives of plants and animals

green bin: a container for organic kitchen and household wastes. The green bin is picked up from the curbside by the local waste collection in some cities and composted for use in gardens. See *blue box, compost.*

greenhouse gases: gases in the atmosphere, such as carbon dioxide and methane, that block the escape of excess heat from Earth, causing the average temperature to rise gradually

hazardous waste: garbage that is dangerous to living things, including most batteries, cans of paint, household cleansers, and pesticides. See *toxic.*

incineration: the burning of garbage in a specialized furnace, reducing the waste to ash and gases. Heat from incineration can be used to create electricity.

landfill: a place that accepts, treats, and buries garbage under and over layers of dirt

litter: garbage or wastepaper thrown carelessly about the environment instead of into an appropriate container *municipal:* under the control of a town, city, or local government

organics: natural materials of plant or animal origin, such as grass clippings, leftover fruits and vegetables, and meat. Organics will break down, decay, and return to Earth.

packaging: a wrapping of plastic, metal, or paper used to contain or protect a product before sale

post-consumer waste: material that has been used and can be reused for another purpose, e.g., newspaper

pre-cycle: reduce the amount of garbage by deciding not to purchase or use a wasteful item. See *refuse.*

recycle: divert materials from the regular garbage and reuse them in the original or a changed form. One of the three R's. See *reduce, reuse.*

reduce: use less in order to cut back on waste. One of the three R's. See *recycle, reuse.*

refuse: choose not to use or buy something, such as an overpackaged toy. See *pre-cycle.*

reuse: keep an item in use rather than waste it, such as giving it to another person. One of the three R's. See *recycle, reduce.*

scavenger: a living organism, such as a vulture, that feeds on dead organic matter. Also, a person who seeks out, collects, and uses things that have been discarded.

toxic: poisonous, dangerous, or hazardous to people and the environment. See *hazardous waste.*

zero waste: recycling all materials back to Nature or to human use so that nothing goes to waste

Actions to Take

RE-think
reduce, reuse, recycle
react, reconsider, redesign, rebate, realign, reply, respond, return
refresh, restart, remodel, rework, repeat, reconnoiter
reinforce, refit, recover, reword
reinstate, recharge, renew, refuel, re-energize, reapply, relocate, redecorate
refuse, renounce, require, reform, renege, regurgitate, reverse, revenge
reject, revolt
remember, rejoice, reveal, rebirth, rediscover, revisit, reward, recreate
*RE*spect

3/92